PRAYERS FOR MY VILLAGE

Michel Bouttier

Translated from the French by
Lamar Williamson

UPPER
ROOM BOOKS
NASHVILLE

�֎ �֎ �֎

Prayers for My Village
an English translation
© 1994 by Lamar Williamson
All rights reserved.

Translated from the French
with the permission and cooperation of the author,
Michel Bouttier.

First published in 1954 by the Community of Pomeyrol;
published in 1982 as *Prières pour mon village*
(copyright "*Edition française*" by Editions Oberlin, 1982).
This English translation is published
with the permission of Editions Oberlin, Strasbourg.

✖ ✖ ✖

Cover Photo: "France, Jura Mountains"
© Nik Wheeler / Westlight
Cover Design: Jim Bateman / Bateman Designs
First Printing: October 1994 (3)
Library of Congress Catalog Card Number: 94–60728

ISBN 0–8358–0711–8
Printed in the United States of America

*For servants of God
and the people of God
in a global village*

Prayer,
the vigil of an insistent presence in a world in gestation,
is more essential than ever.

— Annette Butte
Community of Pomeyrol
France

Translator's Preface

Some years ago a French friend gave me a copy of *Prières pour mon village*, thinking that I would find in the author a kindred spirit. Michel Bouttier's prayers so nourished my soul that I decided to translate the entire little book for my personal use as a way of entering into each prayer.

Here one breathes the air of the French Midi and feels the heartbeat of a Reformed pastor. To pray with Bouttier is to renew spiritual ties that bind the heritage of Huguenots in America to their roots. But that is not all. In the idealism of this young minister; in his struggles as he confronts apathy, failure, sickness, and sin in himself and his parishioners; and above all in the love that unites him with his flock and with the Good Shepherd, we find elements that transcend confessional bounds and surmount the distinction between laity and clergy. These prayers are catholic in the original, broad sense of that term. They give voice to movements of the heart that are universally human.

I have used these prayers in French with students in Africa who have also resonated warmly to the pastor's heart that speaks here. In prayer the distance between continents, cultures, and generations vanishes. We find ourselves together in the presence of God.

�֍ �֍ ✖

The renewal of interest in spirituality in our time has called attention to the fact that few works of Reformed piety are readily available today. Believing that many others will find that these prayers of a young pastor in the Reformed Church of France are, as the French say, *pleines de sève* ("full of sap"), I am glad to play a part in making them available to English-speaking Christians.

Annette Butte, founder of the Protestant Community of Pomeyrol in southern France, first felt the value of these prayers. She published them in 1954 in the series *Cahier de Pomeyrol (2)*.

Forty years later, Michel Bouttier, the young pastor of St. Laurent d'Aigouze, has retired from a distinguished career at the Protestant Seminary in Montpellier, France, where he taught New Testament and edited the journal *Etudes thèologiques et religieuses*. Committed to solid biblical scholarship and Christian engagement in the world, Professor Bouttier continues to write and to serve from his home base, "La Pigne," on a hillside near Puy-St. Martin in the Drôme.

Kananga, Zaïre
March 1994

To Precede the Day

"I will arise before the dawn. . . ."
I will come to precede words and works.

I come, Lord, to precede the awakening of my village,
and all that will be done today
in our houses and our fields.

Before the cock crows, before the Evil One comes,
may You be in this place. Let this day be offered to You,
returned to Your right hand!

I come to call You to look upon and bless us all.
No noise yet, no word, no act: among us, Lord,
may You be always first named, first sought, first served.

Amen.

Prayers for My Village

Part 1

Praise

O Lord, our God,
how majestic is Your name in all the earth!
How majestic is Your name in my village,
despite our infidelities
and the weakness of Your church.

How beautiful it is here, Your name . . .
O village of the plain, more beautiful
than the mountains and the hills,
than snows and glaciers,
than valleys and crags.

O my village,
You are beautiful with God,
beautiful with His presence and His grace,
beautiful with His love.

O my village,
the most beautiful horizon on earth,
since here, for us, the Lord lives!

When the Hail Threatens

Lord,
You call me this night to be like the captain on the bridge
when a tempest overtakes the ship.
You call me to come here on my knees while this new
wave of storm once more threatens the grape harvest.

Morning

O, Lord, be for my village today
a rampart and a fortress! Ward off
the Devil who stalks our streets,
around our houses and in our fields;
protect us from his attacks: abomination,
luxury, envy, jealousy, hatred, pride, disdain . . .
Be Yourself our light, like this light that rises now
and pushes back the darkness of the night.

I hear them hitching up the carts,
the first footfalls echoing on the road.
On the threshold of the day, place me again
at the service of my village.
You know it and love it much more than I.
You know my unworthiness,
but have You not placed me here so that I should be
before You, Lord, at the foot of Your throne,
the constant reminder of its existence?

Noon

At the time when each family finds itself again at table,
and because "man does not live by bread alone,"
I come to seek for my village, Lord, the nourishment of
Your word, and Your benediction.

In the name of all of them,
here are the thanks they do not always
think of offering to You.

Be praised, Lord,
for the bread You give our village
each day so abundantly.

Be praised for each table that is set.
O Lord, be with us all,
at the meal in each house!
Be the host in every home.

Saturday Night

In this happy hour, when the village
tries to forget the weariness of the week
and finds itself on the verge of the Kingdom,
hour of relaxation and preparation,
keep me standing at my post.

Hour of recreation, let the shepherd watch
so that joy may be preserved.
Hour that precedes Your day;
let the shepherd watch so that
Your coming will be greeted.

I pray to You. Here they are . . .
Those who lounge on the doorsteps,
who gather at the family table.
Those who dash off to the movies,
those at the dance, those in the cafés.
Those who love each other and who,
perhaps this night will conceive a child.
Those who hope for and hasten Your coming.

✼ ✼ ✼ ✼

Grant to my village true happiness while awaiting
the joy of Your Kingdom!

Let it remind us of Your invitation, Lord:
the invitation to the Kingdom and, tomorrow already,
the invitation to Your house.

You send me along the streets, across the square,
all the way to the borders of the fields.
You want the festive hall to be filled.
You want us to be constrained to enter
so that no place will remain empty; and here I am, Lord,
with no means of constraint other than a prayer.

Let's go together, then, door to door: here we are, Lord,
    street by street, house by house, family by family,
        each name is called before You.

The circuit is finished.
Everything has been given back to You now;
we are all placed in Your hand.
The coming day is Yours.

Tomorrow, let Your name be hallowed
    and Your kingdom come;
let Your will be done in our village as in heaven.

Amen.
Alleluia!

Why this refusal, O my Savior, to announce Your Word?
Why this dead weight? This headlong flight?
Why these evasions?
Why am I so heavy and so rigid in Your hands?

Restore to me the joy of Your salvation.
Let me announce it with joy and simplicity of heart, and
not as one who sets down a heavy burden.

Prayer of Thanksgiving

Thank You, Lord, for the joy of this Sunday morning.
Thank You for the happiness of seeing these beloved faces
    gathered a few moments before You.
Thank You for the grace of recognizing in them
    Your presence here below.
Thank You for being the risen, living One;
and Your body, wonder of wonders, is us!

Sunday Evening

Lord, grant me now to rest in peace.
Once the seed is sown it grows, You have told me,
whether the sower wakes or sleeps.

As a hen gathers her chicks,
as a shepherd toward evening assembles his flock,
let my prayer gather this village and all Your creatures
here before You, now.

Joy

Grant me today, Lord,
   a new heaven and a new earth.
Grant me the wonder of a child who for the first time
   opens her eyes upon the world;
the joy of a child who discovers
   Your splendor in each object,
in each encountered being,
   a reflection of Your glory.

Grant me the joy of one whose steps are new.
Grant me the happiness of one whose life is each day
fresh and innocent and hopeful, each day pardoned.

Grant me to see everything in Christ —
trees and fields, homes and tasks, animals and people —
and to be thankful,
O my God!

Prayers for My Village

Part 2

Morning

As each morning the shepherd waters his flock, Lord,
I want to lead these sheep to You, the source of life,
so that in You they may have the water of life today.

As each morning the shepherd arises and
    goes toward the mountain, so, Lord,
each morning on my knees,
I want to arise and
    lead my village toward your High Places,
that it may live this day close to You.

Noon

Lord, in the middle of the day,
in the midst of noise and activities;
in this instant of pause, of regrouping,
and of brusque silence outside,
let me also learn to set aside this moment
to gather my village around You,
to find in You rest and repose at noon.

Receive again this hour the praise of Your creation,
the filial respects of Your children.

In the Heat of the Day

Lord, in the heat of this day,
as all are leaving to confront hard labor,
when each one is going off to sulfate* his vines,
I too want to confront Your presence —
  to stand before You for them,
   even if everything makes me dull and drowsy,
    even if it is hard for me to open myself to Your grace
   when the sun beats down and dries up everything.
I want also at this hour to stay at the post entrusted to me.

Thank You for interrupting my projects
to set me again in the essential place
which I repeatedly desert.

To sulfate (sulphate) is to spray a vineyard with a sulfur-based
chemical that kills parasites and mildew which would otherwise
destroy the vines and thus, the harvest. Sulfating is a difficult,
laborious, and dirty – but necessary – job.

Hear, Lord, the sighs of your creation;
it is in labor.
See these days of battle.
Men burned by sun and sulfate,
Vines with drooping leaves, ravaged by mildew,
sapped by the Destroyer.
Horses given over to the bloody assault of flies and
mosquitoes.

Your creation is panting, Lord;
longing to be delivered of this torment.
Grant to it a share in the liberty of Your children:
let it enter into glory.

Its inarticulate complaint becomes a prayer:
Come, Lord Jesus!

Night of Frost

Lord, what a struggle to overcome my old humanity,
shivering and lazy, in order to do battle now.
Lord, it is going to freeze tonight. Consider the threat
that hangs over us all; see the destructive work of the
Evil One. We are all in Your hand. Your will be done,
Lord. Please ward off all danger this night.
If You want to test us, if we are to be ravaged,
then let it be the better to entrust ourselves to Your grace
and the more faithfully to await from You our daily bread.
But do not let the Enemy win the victory.
For Your name's sake.

Lord, You have overcome in me.
You have led me here to my knees, in Your presence.
Let this be for me the guarantee of Your victory for us all.
Tonight.

Amen.

Friday

Lord, let Thy cross be today
the source of a prayer of thanks, of a solace,
of a renunciation, of a victory in my village.
Let there be someone behind a plow, at the dishes,
who remembers it and blesses You.

Here is this hour, at least, which without the cross
would not have been one of love and adoration.

During a Strike

I must seek refuge near You tonight, Lord.
You know my heavy heart, weighed down by this strike.
Look down from heaven, see Your torn Body. Where is
your Church? What has become of our community of
faith? As soon as it's a matter of life, of bread, of work;
as soon as one leaves the church house, where are they,
Your kingdom and power? O Lord, have mercy on us!

Have mercy on my village.
See the rancor, hatred, and divisions that have built up in
    just a few days.
O, deliver us from the Evil One who ravages us!
In this time of Ascension when You call me to celebrate
the lordship of your Son, I am depressed.
What has become of His victory over us? Over my village?

O, that You would part the heavens and come down.

Night

Lord, here I am before You in the silence,
in the name of my village. Your church is at Your feet.

I am the suffering of A.S.,
    who is desperately looking for work.
I am the grief of Mrs. G., the rootlessness of B.,
    on the evening of this funeral.
I am J.B.
    and his responsibility among the sick entrusted to him.
I am these children
    gathered this morning in the communicants' class.

I am this village, bruised and wounded.
I am this impoverished, aging pastor.
There! That is all that I bring
as I bow before You in the silence of the night.

I am this thick shadow that awaits the light.
For their sake,
I need You to accept me now and speak to me.

Prayer of Release

It pierces me, Lord, Your word:
"I have not lost one of those You have given me."

O, do not settle accounts with me, wretched shepherd that
I am — those whom I have left, those who have strayed
alongside me, these children baptized, or these young
people instructed by my ministry who have left us,
these homes visited, this village entrusted.

O Lord, forgive me!
My only comfort is in Your promise:
You will lead them back Yourself,
into Your fold by the paths of mercy that You alone know;
You, the sovereign Shepherd of the sheep.

Insomnia

My God, I want to bless You for keeping me awake like this in the silence of the night. I thank You that my body, in its troubles, forces my indolent soul to seek You like this, that it keeps my soul breathless and needles it into prayer. You know my whole desire would be to sleep, always. It takes all the resources of Your grace to lead me to You and to make of me the pastor of my village, the one who, in the middle of the night, leads all his flock so that it will be brought once more into Your grace. I pray You to keep me like this until I have presented to You all those whom You have entrusted to me.

After that, grant, O Father, the rest which I need.

I want to give myself over to Your inspiration, knowing it is not in vain that I am so belabored by this bodily hindrance. How good it is to be able to praise You at all times and in every way. Alleluia, alleluia!

Prayer for True Love

Lord, save me from affability, that human and
cheap form of love. Keep me from substituting for
Your mercy my friendly feelings, for Your interventions
my indulgent inclinations.
Preserve in the salt of the earth its savor!

Your love desires all that is in me and everything for me.
Do not tolerate this sickly sweet affection that coddles
with a hot compress the wounds of those whom You have
entrusted to me, that justifies them in their own eyes and
delivers them not at all. My affability is a collaboration
with the Evil One — it seeks good personal relations
but betrays You, O my King! I am no longer your servant.

Faithful love — Yours — is not a balm but an operation,
not a compress but an attack,
not a compromise but redemption.

To love my village, O my Savior,
is it not to lay upon it the absolute demand
of Your Kingdom?

Intercession

Lord, here I am this morning before You.
More than watchmen wait for the morning,
I await the revelation of Your face.
I arise before the dawn;
I celebrate You, Eternal God.

Here I am in the name of all my village still asleep.
With them, for them, in the name of all,
in this communion which the Holy Spirit gives,
here we are so that this morning, in the silence, our praise
may ascend from our village, my prayer of adoration,
so that here creation may respond to Your love
and sing the glory of Your Name;
so that here the world may not be dumb
but may intone this Alleluia:
Hosanna! Blessed be the Lord!

Here we are in prayer, the work of Your Holy Spirit,
joined in a common expectancy, in a common love:
the expectation of Your coming, the love of Your name.
Here we are now, one in Your grace;
here we are, bound together indissolubly.
Here is the joy of Your Kingdom!

Lord, here I am with all those I don't know how to talk to,
all those to whom I don't know how to announce Your
reign; here I am with these visits misused,
with these men and women to whom I have been
able to speak no word from You; here I am with them
to say at least something to You from them.

O Lord, since I do not know how to speak to them of You,
may I at least know how to speak to You of them, for them;
to praise You with them, for them; to await Your coming,
in prayer, with them, for them. Amen.

Prayers for My Village

❈ ❈ ❈

Part 3

❈ ❈ ❈

Interment

My soul is troubled. What shall I say?
Father, deliver me from this hour?
Father, glorify Your name!
You know how heavy crying and pain are for me.
I withdraw prudently from trouble so as not to be rattled.
Grant me, Lord, on the contrary,
to give myself over to suffering and to tears.
Let me flee from nothing, but come defenseless and
without armor to receive blows, to endure them and, in
Jesus Christ, to bear them to the end.

For this hour I have come . . .
this hour when Your word must be proclaimed,
this hour when the voice of Your consolation and Your
hope must be heard, when Your love wants to show itself!

Help me, Lord, to be a pastor!

Distress

I am unworthy, Lord,
to be pastor of this village, I the hireling;
unworthy to call, I who have not come;
to preach, I who go off and hide. . . .

Since, against my will, You keep me at my post,
be my refuge, Chief Pastor;
have mercy on me, my Shepherd!

Offering

Lord,
this morning I want to hear what You have to say to *me*.
I do not want always to hold out my hands for my village,
for others, but today for my obedience, my sanctification.

Lord, You see it: I seek to serve You,
but without giving up any of my comforts.
I follow the course of my inclinations;
I flee all that stands in their way.
I love whatever satisfies my own desires;
I dread whatever might cost the true offering of my body.

Fix my gaze on Your cross this morning.
Let Your love alone push and possess me. Constrain me
to sacrificial living. Bring down vanity and reputation.
For the armchair, let Your grace substitute the cross.
Amen. Amen.

Prayer to the Spirit

Holy Spirit, baptize me today. Let Your fire rekindle the instrument that You have chosen. My outer nature destroys itself day after day. According to Your unforgettable promise, continually renew my inner nature. You know the weakness of my body: languor, apathy, sleep. You see, locked in impotence, these gifts of Your grace in me: these revelations, these approaches, these struggles, and these joys. Why these words that stick in my throat? These babblings? These hesitations? Have You lost Your grip on me? Could I be stronger than You in my body? O, triumph over my heaviness!

Let the mass of my flesh not block Your surge; let Your inner coming be translated into deeds and evident signs. Blaze Your trail across my body; cleanse it so it may become a display window; exorcise it so that it will be a bent bow. Yes, Lord, stretch this slack cord till it can finally make Your arrows sing. As a bent bow, so I would like my body to be in Your service!
O, Holy Spirit, make of my whole being
a new creation!

The Low Wind

The low wind has risen this morning.
Its panting troubles the surface of the marshes.
The walls sweat with humidity, and in human hearts rises
what had crouched.

Life is heavy today.
Cast out our demons, Lord, and from the other horizon
cause to blow that vital breath, Your Holy Spirit.

To Be a Child of God

Lord, let me today be docile in Your hand
and at the same time spontaneous;
faithful yet constantly on a new way.
Grant me fullness of obedience and fullness of freedom;
total dependence and total independence;
full submission and full release.
Being out front and behind in that,
following You, I will walk before You.

Let everything in me be
    response and responsibility,
        gratitude and initiative,
            imitation and discovery.

Father, let me be Your child!

Evening

Here I am, Lord,
once more to plead the case of my village before You.
I do not know how to penetrate the opaque veil that
conceals from us the nearness of Your Kingdom.
I do not know how to tear down the artificial decorations
of "religion"; behind them we would find freedom itself,
joy, the glory of Your presence!

O Lord, let me not cease, at least,
to present my village to You.
In prayer let the fog that hinders each and all of us
be dissipated — let that be my ministry!

Before You I have free access;
I have this grace to be able to speak to You about us,
knowing that You hear, that You understand.
Our wretchedness — have You not shared it in Christ?

Appoint me anew to my village
Let nothing in me withdraw from it.
Keep me from evasions,
as if everything would be easier somewhere else,
in town, a mission field.
It's here, Lord, isn't it?
Let my ministry be one not of compromise but of fullness,
holding back neither years nor weeks nor moments.
My village — have You not loved it from all eternity?

Prayer for Completion

Lord, deign to complete the work You have
begun in me; deign to bring it to its fullness.
Do not permit me to love You only halfway.
Cut off that which ought to be cut off.
Punish me if necessary, as a father punishes his child.
Correct, humiliate me in Your love which wants
everything of me, so that I may be without flaw and
without concealment in Your hands,
without murmur or hesitation in my obedience,
whole-hearted and full of joy in my love.
Do not abandon the work of Your hands,
Eternal God.
Do not give up!

Supplication

O Lord, draw me to You.
Let me, with singleness of heart, be stretched toward You.
Let me not turn from You through fascination with the
Evil One. O, I do not want my attention fixed on this evil
which shows itself day after day in my village. O, let me
not be caught and borne down by things avowed or
unavowed, open or hidden, perceptible or invisible:
Draw me to You — yes, let me be stretched
with singleness of heart toward You —
toward You and not toward the dizzying abyss.
Let my eye reflect what I see in You and not what the
Evil One wants to disclose to me of his work.
Give me total purity to travel through this world.
Give me the purity of those who look toward Your heaven
— not in order to escape, not to abandon companions,
but to be a torch of light!

O, draw me to You, my Lord.
Let me be stretched toward Your own holiness.
Grant me to be holy — because You are holy!
O, draw me to You!

Visitation

I praise You, my Savior, for having come like this
to seek me and find me. I praise You for giving me this joy
of Your presence, this happiness of knowing that I am no
longer alone here in my village.

I praise You because You have visited me,
as a friend whom one sees again after a long absence,
as a guard who passes by in the course of his rounds.

I praise You for expecting me here, in my village!

Afternoon

You sent me to make these visits, Lord.
House to house, meeting to meeting,
sharing to sharing I have walked.
And in each one, O Master,
You are the One I have found!

Unjust Judge

Hear, Lord, this woman who for thirty years
has pursued You with her prayer.
Not one day has she ceased to plead with You
on behalf of her husband.
Will you never vindicate her?
She demands for him the bread of life:
will You obstinately give him a hardened rock?

Evening Prayer

Lord, never let me sleep until
I have stretched my hands over my village
and invoked your blessing on it.

Watch over us, eternally!
Amen.

Village Festival

The multicolored crowd has invaded the street
dizzy with dust and sunlight.
I can't help but look for You in the crowd, Lord Jesus:
Is it You who, as on the descending turn from Bethphage,
stir up this exultation?

Here come the black bulls, galloping along at a lively clip:
they are the ones the village hails today.
Don't be jealous; You must not leave the festival,
for of this also You are the Savior.

Parable

It is Sunday. A Sunday in May.

The public square,
surrounded by houses and patios, draws to itself the
extremities of the village streets and alleys.
The ground, already hot,
has been swept and sprinkled with cool water.
In the shade of the sycamores, *pétanque** games
unfold their spectacle of gesture and of word.

The cafés have extended their awnings
then spewed out tables and chairs.
Here someone taps a playing card,
there F. tells his stories that attract a cluster of
caps and square-patterned shirts.

---

pétanque - a game similar to bowling in England, but played
with heavy steel balls on the bare ground. *Pétanque* in France is
the rough equivalent of horseshoes in America.

Through wide-open doors
the Catholic church and the Protestant chapel
empty out strings of women in black and girls in white,
whose double procession curves around the fountain and
meets at the ecumenical *patisserie*.[**] Like martins, the
boys dart quickly in and out on their new bikes.

❨ ❨ ❨

Lord, no doubt I lack ambition and imagination,
but for me this hour has always been
a preface to Your Kingdom.

[**] *patisserie* - a pastry shop.

Praise

Praise to You, Lord, because I am now part of the village!
Praise to You for the inexhaustible joy
of meeting the people to whom You have bound me.
Members of a commune, the crew of a ship.
You want to weave our lives into a single pattern,
struggling together for the harvests of the earth
and for Your coming; companions in a single adventure
here below, heirs of the same Kingdom in eternity.

Praise to You for this double present,
royal gift of Your unique love.

Psalm 130

"Out of the depths I cry to You, O Lord."

In anguish He died,
He whom You loved.
Here we are,
slapped right in the face,
our legs trembling.

Were You not His support, His companion?
Are You no longer here, even
to come touch the edge of His casket?

"He who believes in me will also do
the works that I do, and greater works than these
will he do because I go to the Father."

Is there then no more promise for Your Church?
Will its only ministry be to bury people?
He whom You loved is dead.
A heavy veil is drawn over
the public square, suddenly silent,
and Your Church seeks her Savior. . . .

"My soul waits for the Lord.
More than the watchmen wait for the morning."
Yes, more than the watchmen count on the dawn!

Before the Sermon

It is in spite of myself, Lord,
that I once more have the responsibility
of proclaiming Your word.

You know my ardent prayer: let the weight of my denials
fall on me alone! Let no obstacle exist between these
people and Yourself. Let them not be deprived of true joy
because of their unworthy pastor. Set me aside so You
can speak Yourself, and let each one receive something to
live on for the week, enough bread to abide in You!

O my beloved Savior, fill my heart with love for
this village: I do not want to unload this sermon
but to accomplish it in the fullness of Your love.
Let it be crucified, my sermon, so as to translate the
wisdom of Your grace alone. Answer this expectation for
the sake of my village that needs You to live, for the sake
of that promise You made to me the day You called me.
Amen.

Gethsemane

Olive trees, drawn up like troops
at the gates of the village —
olive trees,
you who watched in the garden that night
and heard that we must not sleep.
Olive trees,
drill us in vigilance
since He is here in agony, the beloved Son of God.
Olive trees,
guards of the Lord that line the road, along with
the black lances of the cedars.

Emmaus

Lord, we had walked a long time without being able to
recognize You. We were going along together, but our
hearts were heavy, heavy with defeat, with hurt feeling,
with fogginess, and with indifference. We were saying as
we walked that it's all over for Your people here and the
stone of the tomb has rolled shut on all our hopes.

Then, this Sunday, You gathered us around the table.
The bread was broken, our eyes were opened,
and we recognized You. . .
this great fraternal circle, so often torn,
Your resurrected Body!

Monologue in the Night

Lord, if I come in the silence of this night, it is not to
grapple again with the election of church officers, the
youth center, my ministry, or my shortcomings — it is so
You can come take possession of what is Yours within me.

As a deer longs for flowing streams,
so longs my soul for You, O living God!
But where shall I find You?
You come, then You withdraw at will.
You ought not to make me come here,
since You are such a reticent God.
You ought not to call me,
since You know that I am a sinner.

You alone can be Pastor of my village,
but You stand aside, and You reject my sin.
You have seduced me; You have deceived me.
You made me believe that I would walk with You,
and I cannot do it.

You made me believe that You would
always be with us — and You are not!
But against You, Lord, I have no other help,
no other defense, save Yourself. . . .
O, come soon!

Your presence, Lord,
is sometimes peaceful and happy
because it is expected, welcomed, adored.
There is also this bitter and tenacious presence
by which You pursue me
when I will not give myself to You.

I have fled from You, Lord,
and yet I have not been at peace for one instant
during all these weeks: Your gaze has been
constantly fixed on me, Your sad gaze.
O grant me, Lord, to know You now
in Your power and Your joy!

Baptism

My Father, what a joy to hold this child in my arms
and to perform, upon its head and in Your name,
the act of baptism!
Praise to You, because all Your promises to us
are "yes" and "amen" in Jesus Christ!
Praise to You for this new life that is born.

Your promise is solemnly sealed today for this child,
as it once was for each of us.
It is sealed as one lays the first stone in the mortar.
It is sealed as one brands an animal in a herd,
as one puts a ring in the nose of a bull from the range.
It is sealed as one seals a precious letter
that no one should open.

Praise to You
because this child is marked to be Your child.
You have promised us this
in the presence of everyone,
a public promise which nevertheless
remains Your secret.

Prayers for My Village

■ ■ ■ ■

Part 4

■ ■ ■ ■

In Time of Sickness

Here is my body, Lord, target of suffering,
stretched out, defenseless, offered as a sacrifice to the
assaults of the night, for this is the hour of darkness.

And now what shall I say? Father, deliver me from this
hour! It is not for this hour that I have come? Am I no
longer pastor of my village? Isn't this my ministry that
continues through this hour? My ministry — not what I
say, but what I am, for them, in Jesus Christ? Is it a matter
of indifference for this parish of which I am pastor that my
body is laid low this evening, given over to suffering and
to grace? "I have been crucified with Christ!"

※ ※ ※

It's You I'm calling, You alone.
Come, Lord, share the suffering
You have given me to offer to You.
In moments of total lucidity,
as in moments of drowsiness,
let suffering remain this night
the very sign of Your presence!

※ ※ ※

May I offer to You, Lord, these hours when there is
nothing, these interminable hours when I am no more
than a waiting body? More than healing, yes, more than
healing, may You be the object of my expectation!

Here, then, is my task this evening,
O Master: not the usual weekly Bible study,
but to be stretched out here, for no good reason,
with nothing to do, tested, tempted,
so that we may be exercised together,
strengthened together in Your fellowship, Lord Jesus!

My God, my Father, I want to bless You from the bottom of my heart. Let all that is in me bless Your Holy Name! I am full, my God, above all that I can say. What have I done for so many blessings? My whole village that thinks of me, surrounds me with its prayers and its love — these countless signs that You have multiplied for me.

O my God, yes! Have I not received hundreds and hundreds of times more than I have left: houses, brothers and sisters, fathers and mothers!
Let all that is in me bless Your Holy Name.

O my Lord, I want to bless You for the state of sickness,
because it is so easy then to be a little child and
to let myself be taken by the hand.
I want to bless You because, stretched out like this,
I am really subjected to Your power, unable to escape
or to do anything other than what You will.
How good it is, O my Savior, thus to be Your servant!
Since, alas, I am not strong enough to obey You always
when I can dispose of my life and my time, I bless You for
giving me these days when I cannot flee. Since in health I
don't know how to be Yours, I bless You for this sickness
when nothing can separate me from Your presence.

Praise be to You, my Savior. Just help me not to take my eyes off You. As You have subjected my body and my will, subject my soul as well to contemplate You continually. As You have brought to obedience my members and my movements, so guide into love all that is in me! Lord, it is good for me to be weak in order to know Your strength; it is good for me to do nothing and to let You do as You will.
My suffering seems insignificant,
but since it is mine, this insomnia, this fevered sweat,
here is all I have to give You; here is what I have become.
And when all of that prevents my praying,
when I turn away and when I drift off to sleep,
accept it all as my ardent supplication for my village.

> We give Thee but Thine own,
> Whate'er the gift may be:
> All that we have is Thine alone,
> A trust, O Lord from Thee.*

---

*English-speaking Protestants might think of "We Give Thee but Thine Own" as a rough equivalent of the well-known French evangelical hymn that Michel Bouttier quotes in the original.

⊞ ⊞ ⊞ ⊞ ⊞

O my Father, may I know how to thank You for the
prayers that have gone up to You on my behalf;
may I know how to bless You because I have never been
abandoned to the power of the Enemy,
but continually borne up to You.
O my God, now I belong to myself less than ever.

These powers that Your children have won back are
doubly Yours. My life belongs to them, who have prayed
for me so much. My recovered powers are for this village
that has begged You for them. O my Savior, let me not rob
them of what they have acquired; let me not rob You of
what You have given them. May I not withhold myself,
either from them or from You.

Here I am, O Father, to do Your will!
This is no longer my offering, for I am no longer my own!
Everything has been taken from me, everything returned,
so that I may, through You, live a new life.
Amen.

Convalescence

O our Father, we bless You
for gathering us before You in this hour, despite the
distances that separate us, to adore You.
Grant us, O Father, Your Spirit, so that in all our struggles
we may never doubt Your love, so that in our trials we may
never be torn from Your presence.

Just as we are,
we offer ourselves to You
and pray that always and in every way
our lives may glorify You.
Praise be to You for Jesus Christ,
our Savior and friend, in whom we are united
to one another and to You, forever.
Amen.

Prayer of the Parish

Grant us, Lord, to be like an airfield for this village,
constantly ready to receive You: the land cleared,
the runway constantly retraced and leveled,
where You might, at any moment, come to us and visit us
from on high, assuring us of Your presence,
Your love, Your sovereignty.
Amen.

Parish Offering

Here I am, Lord: I am the offering of the parish.
With their work, their money, they feed me.
They do what they can so I can be there, to pray to You.
My life is their offering to You.
For their sake, accept me.
Forgive me for continually taking
myself back from them and from You:
from them who have called me,
from You who have redeemed me.

Lord, at least in the work of prayer
let me accomplish the task which You
have entrusted to me.
Amen.

Praise to You, Lord, for the Elders of the Church.
Praise to You for Your faithfulness which from age to age,
across the ups and downs of history, has not ceased to call
together here those who would serve You.
I praise You today for H. and the wisdom of his faith
ripened in following the plow.
Praise to You for L. and his hearty joviality which, like a
chestnut, encloses the fruit of his baptism.
Praise to You for V. and this reflective, measured decision
which has led her to You.
Praise to You again for G. — where You have got through
to him, he is solid as a rock.
Praise to You for Your Church here,
flesh of our flatland flesh,
flesh of Your flesh, O Son of God!

Prayer for Jesus

Lord, I have finished my prayer,
and here You draw me back to my knees
to call my thoughts back to You,
to You alone, beloved Savior.
It's Your spirit that moves me —
strangely enough — to pray for You.
I wouldn't dare Lord, but it's Your Holy Spirit who, in me,
urgently demands that You be worshipped and praised.
I beg and implore, for You, the gratitude of
those You came to love and to redeem.

Are You not, for us, "in agony until the end of the world"?
Are You not our intercessor before the Father?
Your suffering with our sufferings, Your humiliation from
our disdain, from our indifference, Your rush of love to see
us gathered together . . .

O Son of God, our Brother, I beseech the Father, who
alone holds the secret, that Your hour may finally come!

Trinity

I discern You, O Father, leaning over this world whose
horizon and whose light You have created. You enfold it
with such love that, for this world, You prepare the
sacrifice of Your son, Your only begotten.

I see You, O Jesus,
arms outstretched on a cross raised in the village square,
You pour out for this village a particular drop of Your
blood so that Your pardon may taken root here.

I watch for You, O Holy Sprit, wind that restores life in the
overpowering heat of summer. As in the first days, as on
Pentecost, You seek here the body which You will make
Your dwelling-place.

Lord, it's not my fantasies, my solicitations, my refusals,
or my desires I am coming to look for this dawn.
I'm sick of them, as You well know.
It's You, O my God — Father, Son, and Holy Spirit —
You whose thoughts are not my thoughts
and whose ways are not my ways.
I don't want to find myself alone with myself
one more time —
    nor even with my village, its problems, its concerns.
It's You I'm waiting for,
no longer the boss to whom one reports in line of duty, but
You, for the love of Your Name, for Your own sake alone!

My soul thirsts for You, O living God.
It's Your Holy Spirit, O my God, who comes
and hollows out this expectant space within me.
It's Your doing that my heart says to me:
　　　　Seek the face of the Lord.
And I do seek Your face, O God of my salvation!
I thirst for You. The closer You are —
the more Your presence surrounds me —
the more lively and ardent is this thirst.

I thirst for You, because Your Holy Spirit comes in me
　　— with sighs too deep for words —
to breathe the expectation of all Your creatures,
comes to sing what I could not otherwise know;
springs up in me like the first spark of Your Kingdom.
I have a divine thirst for this journey, its customary task,
the youth to instruct, the sick to visit.

I have a divine thirst for the wind which is rising.
I have a divine thirst for each word, each gesture,
each thought. I thirst for You in all my being —
my spirit, my soul, and my body.
I thirst for You for S. and for my little P.
I thirst for You.

This is not a covetous desire, an appetite of my pride.
It is the gift of Your Spirit! Alleluia!
I thirst for You for all my village, and, for it, I come to
draw with joy from the wellspring of salvation.
My soul thirsts for You, O living God!

Lord, teach me to turn toward You,
even if I don't yet know how to look at You.

Lord, You are my strength,
even if I don't know how to grasp You.

Lord, You are my salvation,
even if I don't know how to believe.

Lord, You are my pardon,
even if I no longer know how to repent.

Lord, You are love,
even if I don't know how to love.

Praise be to You!

Prayer to Be True

Lord, let the pattern of my life,
    the course of my days,
be inexplicable apart from the intervention
       of the Risen One.
Let Jesus Christ be the sole justification
    for my life.

All Creatures of Our God and King

All you inhabitants of my village, praise the Lord!
Praise Him, young and old;
Praise Him, poor and rich, workers and owners,
and you Catholics and Protestants.
Praise the Lord, you who labor under the sulfate;
Praise Him, women, in your never ending housework.
Praise Him, children, through your compositions
  and your math problems. Praise the Lord,
you who pass in the streets and on the square.
Praise Him, you who are seated in the cafés.
Praise Him, merchants behind your counters.
Praise the Lord, craftsmen in your workshops.
Praise, Him, pastor and priest.
Praise to You, O my Savior,
at home, in our fields, and our dwellings.
Praise to You in Your house.
May all our toil find here its reward and its fulfillment
so as to become song and praise.
May our sheaves be bound together now
and carried to You.
                              Hosanna!

✠ ✠ ✠

Benediction: Travel Permit

May you each day and every moment, in the
fellowship of Jesus' sufferings and sharing His
feelings, bury all that threatens to confound you in
your ministry. May you be granted each moment to
measure up to His pardon, His power, and to the
royal achievement of love — and thus, half hidden,
half visible, to see traced across the enigmatic
geography of your parish, the real foundation of the
Kingdom of God.

✠ ✠ ✠

From a letter on the
Eve of ordination to the gospel ministry

The Author

Michel Bouttier served a total of twenty years as pastor to churches in the Eglise Reformée de France (French Reformed Church). He was for a decade professor in the Faculté de théologie protestante, Montpellier, France, where he taught New Testament studies.

He received degrees from the University of Grenoble, the University of Strasbourg, and earned his doctorate at the Faculté de théologie protestante, Montpellier.

Bouttier is a prolific writer whose popular and scholarly books, including a recent commentary on Ephesians, are widely known in the French-speaking world. One of his early works was translated into English as *Christianity According to Paul* and enjoyed much popularity in the U.S.

He lives in Puy-St. Martin (Drôme), France.

The Translator

Lamar Williamson, friend and colleague of the author, is Professor Emeritus of Biblical Studies, Presbyterian School of Christian Education, Richmond, Virginia. He holds degrees from Davidson College; Union Theological Seminary in Virginia; Faculté de théologie protestante, Montpellier; and Yale University.

He is ordained in the Presbyterian Church (USA). After a pastorate in the United States, he served ten years (1956–1966) as evangelistic/teaching missionary to the Belgian Congo/Zaïre, returning there in 1992–1994 to teach at the Kasaï Reformed Seminary. His many articles, in French as well as in English, deal with biblical and cross-cultural themes. His books include *Mark* in the INTERPRETATION commentary series and *Ishaku: An African Christian Between Two Worlds.*

He lives in Montreat, North Carolina.